# A Dollar a Day

Written by Nancy O'Connor
Illustrated by Walter Carzon

Flying Start
to Literacy®

# Contents

# Chapter 1

# Mickey's new job

Mickey's stomach churned with worry as he hurried down the street towards the coal mine. He had never had a job before. It was five-thirty in the morning and he had to be at the mine by six, so he picked up his pace. It wouldn't do to be late on his first day. He couldn't lose this job.

Mam nearly squeezed the life out of him when he left the house. She held him tight and whispered, "I wish you were headed to school, Mickey, but that's not to be anymore. The girls and I are counting on you, so take good care of yourself." He squirmed out of her hug, grabbed his lunch bucket and mumbled goodbye as he hurried out the door.

Mickey had gone to the one-room schoolhouse on the edge of town for five years. Miss Prentice was the only teacher he'd ever had, and he liked her a lot. Yesterday she told him he was the best 11-year-old pupil she'd ever had, in both arithmetic and reading. Mickey's cheeks had grown hot from her praise. But then he'd said, "Today's my last day of school, Miss Prentice."

"Oh, dear, Mickey! Why is that?"

"I'm going down in the mine tomorrow. I got a job as a mule boy," he explained. "I have to – on account of my dad dying." He thought he saw her brush a tear away, but he wasn't sure.

Mickey had never been inside the mine before. Today
he'd take the cage down the Number Three shaft of the
Deer Run Colliery. His heart thumped like a drum. He
hated feeling so scared. His dad had told him how dark
it was 300 metres below ground. There were the rats
down there, too, big as cats. And gas that could kill a
man with just a whiff or two. Dad had never wanted
Mickey to go underground, but someone had to support
the family. It was his job now.

He got in line with the miners and other mule drivers, and when the iron cage opened, he squeezed inside. The cage started to descend, and with every creak and lurch, Mickey jumped. The only light came from a dim, flickering bulb dangling from the ceiling of the cage. Thinking about the darkness in the mine made it hard for Mickey to breathe. The other boys stared at him and nudged each other. He knew he stood out – he was the cleanest person in the cage. Everyone else wore clothes stiff with coal dust and caked with dried mud.

One miner leaned down and said, "You Sean Flannery's boy?"

"Yes, sir."

He squeezed Mickey's shoulder. "We were all sure sorry about the explosion. It was mighty brave how your dad went back in to rescue his trapped buddy."

"Thank you, sir."

It had only been three months, but Mickey was having a hard time recalling what his dad looked like. Sometimes he slept with one of his dad's shirts. It helped him remember. It smelt like the peppermints his dad had kept in his pocket as treats for Mickey and his sisters.

Mam was trying to pay the rent on their company-owned house by taking in boarders, but the money she made wasn't enough. The mine owner offered Mickey a job as a mule driver, even though he wasn't as old as he should be. Most of the drivers were 13 or 14.

Mickey felt proud, though. He'd be making a whole dollar a day! Maybe, in a couple of years, he'd have a team of mules and be making a man's wages.

The cage clanged against the wall of the shaft, and Mickey jumped again. To his dismay, a book fell out of his pocket. It was a new novel, *The Stolen Pay Train*. One of the older boys snatched it up. "What do we have here? A book? Look, this school boy brought a book with him." The mule drivers snickered. A few men did, too.

"Thinks he's going to have time to read," the boy said. "In the dark!" He tossed the book back to Mickey.

Another boy spoke up. "School Boy here won't last a week." Mickey wondered if he was right. But as everyone piled out of the cage at the bottom of the shaft, the miner who had been kind to him gave Mickey a pat on the back. "You'll get used to all this, son."

Will I? he wondered.

Near the shaft, a stable had been carved out of rock. The stablemaster nodded to Mickey and pointed to a stall where a mule stood dozing. "That one's yours. His name is Zeke. Get to work," he said.

Mickey looked around. Piles of hay, buckets of water, pitchforks, curry combs and dandy brushes were stowed there for the care of all the mules. He had heard that many of the animals spent their whole lives in the mines, never seeing sunshine or breathing fresh air.

"Last week Zeke kicked his driver, a kid named Ambrose," the stablemaster continued. "Broke his leg in three places. He'll probably always walk with a limp."

Just his luck to get stuck with a bad-tempered mule. Mickey had pulled up two thin carrots from Mam's backyard garden this morning. He hoped she wouldn't notice. They were tucked in his jacket pocket. He thought they would help him make friends with his mule.

## Chapter 2

# Meeting Zeke

"How will I know what to do?"  Mickey asked the stablemaster.  "Who's going to show me?"

"Ask Zeke," the man said.  "He's been down here for four years.  But watch out for him.  He's a difficult one."

Ask a mule?  Mickey kept silent.

Mickey filled Zeke's feed trough with hay. He then set to work brushing the animal's brown coat with a dandy brush. The mule turned his head, rolled his eyes around and glared. He showed his big brown teeth and switched his tail. Mickey stayed away from Zeke's rear end. He didn't want to get kicked on his very first day. He also didn't much care for the wet, stinking pile of straw on the floor of Zeke's stall.

He wrinkled his nose.

"Phew! That smells so bad it makes my eyes water," he said to no one in particular.

"Pays to tie your kerchief over your nose when you muck out the stall," one of the drivers said. "I'm Joe."

"Thanks, Joe. I'm Mickey."

"I think I'll call you School Boy. I'd leave that book at home from now on."

"It's a great book," Mickey said. "You can borrow it when I'm done."

"No, thanks," Joe said. "I don't read books."

Mickey watched how the other boys harnessed their mules, but when he tried to slip on Zeke's harness, the mule bit him. "Ouch!" he yelped. He rolled back the sleeve of his thick denim jacket and could see red welts coming up on his arm. Everyone around him chuckled.

"Zeke's trying to teach School Boy how to do things right," Joe called out.

Joe nudged Mickey in the ribs as he passed by. "Sure hope we don't have a cave-in today. Seems we have one every time a new driver joins up."

Was Joe pulling his leg? Mickey got on with his work, but he sure hoped nothing bad would happen in the mine today.

Mickey noticed raw spots on the mule's back. "Look at these sores on Zeke's back."

"Ambrose didn't take good care of Zeke. That's probably why he got kicked," a driver told him. "Use some liniment on the sores." He tossed a small tin can to Mickey. Mickey scooped some out with his finger and carefully rubbed the animal's wounds. When he tried again to harness Zeke, the mule stood still and cooperated.

"That Zeke is a smart mule," Joe said. "In fact, he's smarter than Ambrose ever was." When he laughed, Mickey joined in. But then he recalled poor Ambrose with his broken leg.

All morning, Mickey sat on the front bumper of his wagon, watching, listening and learning, as Zeke plodded after the other wagons down the dark gangways to where the men were working. If a mule was being stubborn, a driver would crack his black leather snake whip over the animal's head. It made a loud, cracking noise. Mickey had left his whip in Zeke's stall, but he would take it home at the end of the day and learn how to use it.

In the low tunnels, Mickey had to climb down from the wagon and walk. He eyed Zeke warily, fearing another bite. The mule stared back, eyes glowing in the feeble lamplight. Each seemed to be taking the other's measure.

"Keep a sprag handy," one of the drivers told Mickey. He held up a big stick. "Then if your mule tries to squeeze you against the wall, you can smack him with it." Mickey knew sprags were used to brake the coal wagons, but he'd never thought he might need one as a weapon against a mean mule.

The miners filled the wagons with coal, then the boys hitched them together in a long line to be hauled up through the tunnel to the surface. There they would be unloaded. Mickey watched in wonder as a six-mule team pulled 15 filled wagons up the ramp towards the mouth of the mine.

"Don't stand around, kid!" shouted the stablemaster. "If you want to keep your job, get your mule back to work."

It amazed Mickey that Zeke knew his way through the dark and twisting passages of the mine. The mule also sensed when to duck his big brown head to avoid the low ceilings in some of the tunnels. Several times, when Mickey wasn't paying attention, he slammed his forehead into low-hanging rocks. And Joe laughed each time.

"Keep your eye on Zeke, and he'll let you know when to duck," one driver told him. "Mules use their long ears to feel how high the roof is." He showed Mickey his mule's ears. The tips had been worn off. "That happens to lots of them."

Joe could have told me this, thought Mickey, when he saw me hit my head the first time. Joe seemed to enjoy watching him get hurt!

## Chapter 3

# A miner's life

When the drivers stopped a few hours later to eat, Mickey gulped down huge bites of his sandwich. Mam had made him a big lunch – a sandwich, an apple, a piece of miner's cake and a flask of cold tea. The fried egg in his sandwich was cold and stiff between the thick slices of bread, but he didn't care. He was starving.

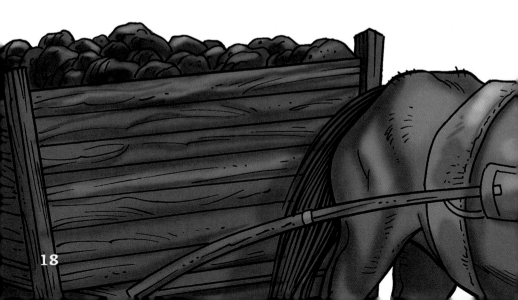

Mickey saw Zeke's big dark eyes staring at him. He remembered the carrots in his pocket. Zeke curled back his lips and grabbed the carrot in his teeth. He ground up the carrot and swallowed it. He stared again at Mickey.

"How'd you know I have another one? You are pretty smart. But I'm saving it for quitting time – if you do good work the rest of the day." He rubbed Zeke's forehead, and the mule nodded, seeming to understand.

Mickey stowed his lunch bucket on a high, rocky shelf and got back to work.

The afternoon dragged on. Mickey wondered what time it was, so he stopped and dug his dad's watch out of his inside jacket pocket. Mam had given it to him after the funeral. He peered at the face of the watch in the dim light.

"I'll take that pocket watch right now!" the boss shouted. Mickey jumped and nearly dropped the watch.

"Sir, it was my dad's. I'll put it away."

"Watches aren't allowed down here," the man scolded. "You should only be thinking about the number of coal wagons you're hauling, not what time it is. If I ever see that watch again, it's mine."

"I ... I won't ever bring it again, sir," Mickey stammered. He was shaking as he slipped the watch back into his pocket. The things he treasured, like his dad's watch and books, were no use in the mine.

In some of the tunnels, he had to wade through mud or knee-deep water. The lamp on his cap did little to light the blackness around him. He got so lost that he just followed Zeke. He hoped that what Joe had said about the mule's intelligence was true and that he wasn't making fun of him again.

How many more trips do I have to make today?
Mickey thought, as he hitched Zeke to another empty
coal wagon.  Suddenly, the mule stiffened his legs
and refused to budge.

"Come on, you stubborn old creature," he shouted.
Zeke laid back his ears and wouldn't move.

"Hey, Joe," he called down the dim tunnel.  "Zeke here
won't move."

"That's because it's quitting time," Joe laughed.  "I told
you a mule is smarter than any school boy.  The mules
know better than we do."

Mickey tried to smile.  He couldn't believe it.  Everyone tells me how smart I am, he thought.  But here, in the mine, a mule is smarter than me.

The other boys were unharnessing their animals and filling troughs with hay and water.  The ones who had teams of four or six mules had many more mouths to feed and coats to brush.  Sure, they made more money, but right now, Mickey was glad he only had Zeke to worry about.  He was cold, wet, exhausted and he smelt like a sweaty mule himself.

## Chapter 4

# Mule boy

By Friday, Mickey was beginning to feel a little like a real mule boy. The bruise from Zeke's bite had turned from purple to yellow, and he'd learnt that the mule liked sugar cubes more than carrots. The minute Mickey arrived in the stable, Zeke began nosing around for treats. The mule's sores from the harness had begun to heal, too, and his brown coat gleamed from the brushing Mickey gave him every morning and night. Mickey felt like Zeke was becoming a friend.

He still brought his book underground but he made sure to keep it well hidden in his jacket. He could not forget the words of his teacher – he was the best 11-year-old pupil she'd ever had.

Mickey no longer felt scared going down in the cage each morning. Still, he couldn't say he liked the darkness or the constant creaking of the wooden beams overhead or the booming explosions that shook him to the soles of his feet. The blasting explosions always made Mickey think of his dad and it filled him with dread that the tunnel where he stood could collapse. But there had been no cave-ins all week, and he and Zeke were hauling ten wagons of coal a day. Every night he washed off the coal dust with soap. When he had been in school, Mickey only had to wash on Saturday, but now that he worked in the mine, he had to wash every day.

"Miss Prentice asked about you when I saw her today," Mam said.

"Book learning doesn't mean much when you're a miner. It's experience that counts."

"Your dad always wanted you to get an education."

Mickey sighed. "Mam, I know how to read, and all the other drivers make fun of me for it." He didn't tell her that one of them, Joe, calls him School Boy.

## Chapter 5

# School Boy

The day began like any other. Mickey hitched Zeke to his wagon and followed the other drivers down the gangway. The miners were working in a different part of the mine, and the tunnels were unfamiliar to the boys. Water dripped down the back of Mickey's neck as he walked beside his mule.

Zeke seemed to be in an especially bad mood that morning, rolling his eyes and snorting at every sound. It made Mickey feel uneasy.

The groaning of the wooden girders overhead sounded like ghosts crying in the night. Mickey thought of his dad. The old-timers said the spirits of dead miners haunted the mines. Was his dad here? Watching him? Warning him? Mickey shuddered and plodded after Joe and the others.

"Hurry up, boys!" the boss shouted. "Get your wagons over here so the men can get them loaded. There's a lot of coal to haul here!"

One of the miners began to shovel coal into the back of Mickey's wagon. Zeke stomped his hooves and shook his head as the coal dust swirled around them. "Hey, calm down, Zeke," Mickey said, stroking the animal's neck. When the wagon was full, he grabbed Zeke's reins, backed the wagon down the gangway to a wide spot, turned it around, then headed back the way they had come. Only Joe was ahead of him, barely visible in the light of his headlamp.

"Wait for me, Joe," Mickey called. "Are you sure you're going the right way?"

"Sure, I'm sure," Joe replied. "Which of us has been working in this here mine for three years? This is a shortcut I know. Just follow me, School Boy."

"But … but look at the sign." Mickey pointed.

The sign said, "DO NOT ENTER! UNSTABLE GIRDERS. KEEP OUT!"

"This is the shortest way to the ramp, School Boy. Get a move on."

Mickey tried again. "The sign says it's dangerous, Joe."

Joe's laughter floated back to Mickey. "Working in the mines is dangerous."

Mickey heard loud creaking from overhead, then another blasting explosion in the distance. Zeke stopped in his tracks.

"Zeke doesn't like this," he called at Joe's back.

"Twist his ear, then."

Mickey looked at Zeke, and the mule looked back. All around him it sounded like the earth was moaning. A low rumble started from somewhere up ahead of him – where Joe had gone. A huge cloud of coal dust billowed down the gangway and enveloped Mickey and Zeke. Mickey's worst fear was happening – the ceiling ahead of them was collapsing.

"Joe! Joe!" Mickey screamed, as he ducked beneath the wagon.

"Help me, Mickey! We're trapped."

When the dust cleared, Mickey stood back up, trembling and terrified. Suddenly he thought of his dad. He dropped Zeke's reins and put his hand on his mule's neck. "Stay here, boy. I have to go help." He grabbed his sprag and ran down the gangway. He could see Joe beside his coal wagon. Huge chunks of rock surrounded him.

Digging with the sprag, Mickey pried up one rock after another and rolled them out of the way. Finally he could grab Joe's pant legs. He leaned back and pulled with all his might. Slowly, Joe emerged from under the wagon. By the light of his headlamp, Mickey could see a gash across Joe's forehead and his face was covered with blood. He reached under Joe's arms and dragged him to where Zeke stood. He slung Joe over the mule's back, unharnessed Zeke from the wagon and turned around, heading back the way they had come.

Mickey let Zeke lead the way, but it seemed to take forever to get back to the stable. The stablemaster helped get Joe into the cage to lift him out of the mine. Mickey rode up with him. Joe mumbled something, and Mickey knelt down so he could hear. "Next time I will listen to you, School Boy. You are brave *and* smart."

The next day, the other drivers slapped Mickey on the back and praised him for saving Joe. He blushed with pride. He really did fit in now, he thought. After Joe recovered and returned to the mine, he did not call him School Boy anymore.

"Guess I should learn how to read, huh?" Joe grinned. "Then I could read danger signs!"

"I could teach you to read," said Mickey, showing him the book he still kept inside his jacket. "I've brought it to work with me every day."

Joe laughed. "Well, maybe I could learn to read a book or two and be as smart as you one day."

# Glossary

**colliery**      a coal mine and the buildings near it

**curry comb**      a comb that slides onto the hand; used to loosen dirt

**dandy brush**      a brush made of stiff bristles; used to remove dirt

**girder**      a large beam used in construction

**headlamp**      an oil-wick cap lamp shaped like a small kettle, providing light to work by

**kerchief**      a piece of cloth worn around the neck

**liniment**      a liquid ointment applied to relieve sores

**shaft**      an opening in a mine that connects the surface to the underground

**stablemaster**      the person in charge of the stables where mules are kept

# A note from the author

When I started to write this story, I knew nothing
about coal mines or the people who worked in them.
I imagined my character Mickey, to be an 11-year-old boy
of Irish immigrants whose family had settled
in the coal mining area of Pennsylvania in the United
States.  But I had to learn what kind of jobs men and
boys did in the mines, what the dangers were, what the
workers were paid, what they ate and many other things.
I was shocked to learn that some mules spent their entire
lives underground.

When you are writing fiction, research is important if
you want your story to have interesting details and sound
realistic.  You may not use all the facts you learn, but
facts can enrich a fictional story.